A ROOKIE BIOGRAPHY

ROBERT LOUIS STEVENSON

Author of A Child's Garden of Verses

By Carol Greene

CHILDRENS PRESS®
CHICAGO

Robert Louis Stevenson (1850-1894)

Library of Congress Cataloging-in-Publication Data

Greene, Carol.
    Robert Louis Stevenson / by Carol Greene.
      p. cm.—(A Rookie biography)
    Includes index.
    ISBN 0-516-04265-3
    1. Stevenson, Robert Louis, 1850-1894—Biography—Juvenile literature.
    2. Authors, Scottish—19th century—Biography—Juvenile literature.
    [1. Stevenson, Robert Louis, 1850-1894. 2. Authors, Scottish.] I. Title.
    II. Series: Greene, Carol. Rookie biography.
    PR5493.G67   1994
    828′.809—dc20
    [B]   94-11944
                                         CIP
                                         AC

Robert Louis Stevenson
was a real person.
He was born in 1850.
He died in 1894.
Stevenson wrote
adventure books for
older children and poems
for younger children.
This is his story.

TABLE OF CONTENTS

"Smout" (top right) grew up in the city of Edinburgh (below).
At top left is the door of his house in Edinburgh.

Chapter 1

Day and Night

All the people he loved
called him Smout.
Smout means "small fry"
in Scottish, and
Robert Louis Stevenson
was a very small boy.

He was often a sick boy too.
He had coughs and colds
and his chest hurt.
Sometimes his ears hurt
and he had to wrap a
warm cloth around them.

But Smout still had fun—
during the daytime.

His pretty young mother
played with him.

His nurse, Cummy,
told him stories
and took him for walks
in the cold, windy city
of Edinburgh, Scotland.

Edinburgh looked like the pictures above and below left
when Robert Louis Stevenson lived there. His nurse
Cummy (below right) took him for walks around the city.

Sometimes Smout's father
worried too much about
things like religion.
But he could laugh too,
and Smout loved him.

Smout even had fun
when he was sick
and had to spend
the day in bed.

He just took his toy soldiers
and his ships and houses
and trees to bed with him.
There he sat and pretended
to be a giant.

But when night came,
Smout didn't have fun.
When he was sick,
he coughed all night.
And when he slept,
he had bad dreams.

Once Smout dreamed
that he had to swallow
the whole world.
He never forgot that dream.

Sometimes Smout
woke up screaming.
Then his father would come
and tell him stories
until he could sleep again.

Robert Louis Stevenson
at age fourteen

Many years later, when
Smout was an adult,
he wrote a poem
about going to sleep:

"The strangest things are there for me,
Both things to eat and things to see,
And many frightening sights abroad
Till morning in the land of Nod."

Sometimes Smout's parents sent
him to his grandfather's house
for fresh, country air.

Roses covered the walls
of Grandfather's house
and a swing hung
from a tree.
Flowers filled the garden
and a stream rushed by.

Smout's cousins visited
Grandfather too, so Smout
had children to play with.

Aunt Jane was
kind to Smout

And kind Aunt Jane
took care of everyone.

Maybe Smout remembered
those days in the country
when he wrote this poem:

"The world is so full of
    a number of things,
I'm sure we should all be
    as happy as kings."

13

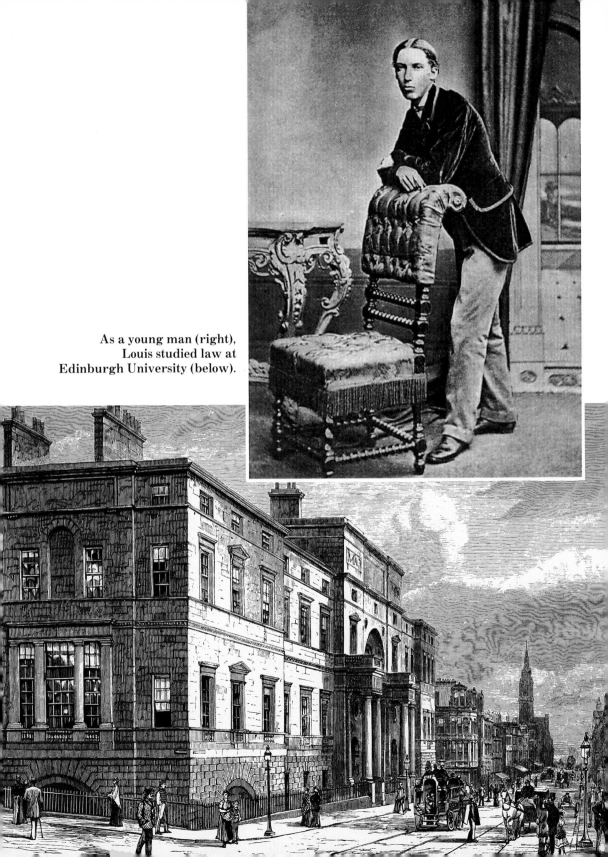

As a young man (right),
Louis studied law at
Edinburgh University (below).

Chapter 2

Learning to Write

When Smout was little,
he didn't go to school
as much as other children
because of his sicknesses.
But he had teachers at home.

Then, when he was a
young man, he went
to Edinburgh University.
By that time, people
called him Louis.

A street in Edinburgh as it looked when Louis was young

Many men in Louis' family
were engineers who
worked with lighthouses.
They wanted Louis
to be an engineer too.

But Louis didn't work
hard at his studies.
He liked to roam around
the shabby parts
of Edinburgh instead.
And he liked to write.

Louis at age twenty-one

At last, when he was 21,
Louis told his father that
he wanted to be a writer.

His father understood.
But he said that Louis
must also study law.
Then, if writing didn't work,
he could become a lawyer.

18

So Louis studied law.
But he worked harder
at his writing.
He thought that writers
had to *learn* to write well.
And he wanted to be
a good writer.

Soon, some of the things
that Louis wrote
came out in magazines.
People liked his writing.

Louis' health was still bad,
so sometimes he went
to other countries.
He hoped different weather
would make him feel better.

In France, Louis went on
a trip with a donkey.
Then he wrote about
his adventures in a book,
Travels with a Donkey.
That book came out in 1879.

In France, Louis also
fell in love with an
American woman, Fanny.
But she was married.
Louis didn't know what
he was going to do.

Fanny Stevenson

Chapter 3

An Island and a Garden

After a while, Fanny
went back to America.
Then she sent for Louis.
She got a divorce and
in 1880, they were
married in California.

Louis was happy now.
Fanny's little boy, Lloyd,
lived with them and
Louis loved him too.

But Louis' health grew worse.
Most people thought
he had tuberculosis.
Tuberculosis hurts the lungs.
In those days,
it killed many people.

So the Stevensons went
from place to place,
looking for one where
Louis would feel better.

Stevenson wrote "Forest Notes" at a small hotel in Barbizon, France.

Louis' father gave him money.
But Louis had to work too.
Besides, he *wanted* to write.

One summer in Scotland,
Louis and Lloyd drew
a map of an island
with buried treasure on it.
They did it just for fun.
But it gave Louis an idea.

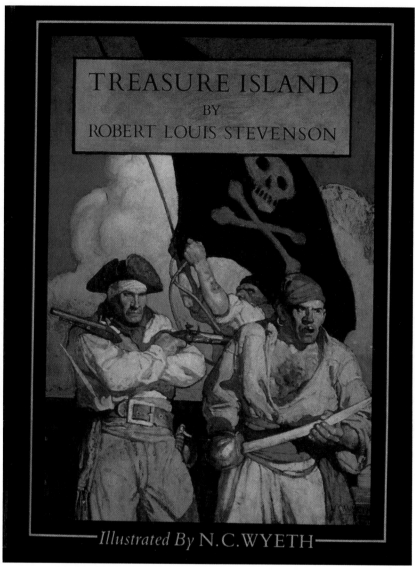

Treasure Island is Stevenson's most famous story.

Soon that idea turned into
a book, *Treasure Island*.
It tells the story of a boy,
a man named Long John Silver,
and a lost treasure.

Scenes from *Treasure Island* show the young hero, Jim Hawkins
(left), meeting a crazy old sailor, and men escaping from
the sailing ship in a small boat (right).

The book came out in 1883
and did very well.

That same summer,
Louis wrote some poems.
Part of him always
felt like a child, so
he wrote them for children.

Illustrations from *A Child's Garden of Verses*

During the next few years,
Louis added more poems.
Then, in 1885, *A Child's
Garden of Verses* came out.
In it were 64
wonderful poems.

"How do you like to go
    up in a swing,
Up in the air so blue . . ."

That poem *feels* like swinging.

"Faster than fairies,
　　faster than witches,
Bridges and houses,
　　hedges and ditches . . ."

That poem *feels* like
riding on a fast train.

Louis dedicated the book
to his old nurse, Cummy.

"From the sick child,
　　now well and old,
Take, nurse, the little
　　book you hold!"

But he had poems in it
for his mother
and Aunt Jane too.

Left: Louis' stepson Lloyd, Fanny, and Louis (left to right) on the porch of their cottage (below) in Saranac, New York.

Chapter 4

A Dream Come True

In his dedication to Cummy
in *A Child's Garden of Verses*,
Louis said he was
"now well and old."
But he was really just 35
and he wasn't very well.

So the family kept moving:
from France to England,
from England to America.
Someplace in the world
must be right for Louis.

Of course, Louis kept writing.
In 1886, *Kidnapped* came out.
It's an exciting adventure
story for older children.

*The Strange Case of
Dr. Jekyll and Mr. Hyde*
came out in 1886, too.
It's a spooky book for adults.

In this scene from
*The Strange Case of
Dr. Jekyll and Mr. Hyde,*
Dr. Jekyll drinks
a drug and becomes
a monster.

The Stevensons were freezing
in New York State when
a man Louis knew
came to him with an idea.

This man would pay for
Louis and his family to
travel around islands in
the South Seas on a yacht.
All Louis had to do was
write letters for newspapers.

The Stevensons on their yacht
in the South Seas. Louis' mother
(left) went along on the trip.

"Yes!" said Louis.
Fanny went to California
to find a yacht.
In 1888, they began their trip.
Louis' father had died,
so Louis' mother went too.

The trip to the South Seas was a dream come true for Louis.

For Louis, it was like
a dream come true.
In *A Child's Garden
of Verses* he had written:

"I should like to rise and go
Where the golden apples grow;
Where below another sky
Parrot islands anchored lie."

Now he was on his way.

Above: The South Sea islands have beautiful beaches and palm trees.
Below: A tiny village on a beach in Samoa. The Samoan people
(inset) were warm and friendly.

Chapter 5

Home

The South Sea islands
were even better
than Louis had hoped.

He liked the flowers and trees,
the mountains and lakes,
the weather, and the people.
Best of all, he felt better,
much better.

The Stevensons' home on the island of Upolu in Samoa.
Inset: Louis playing a flageolet, a small instrument like a flute.

By 1891, the Stevensons
had built a home on an
island in Samoa.
It was big and blue
with a big red roof.
Louis had found his place.

For the next few years,
Louis worked outside and
wrote more books.
He made plenty of money
and he felt fine.

Robert Louis Stevenson (seated) shown with (left to right)
his stepson Lloyd, Count von Vurmbrandt, and the Samoan
chief Tui-ma-le-alii-fano.

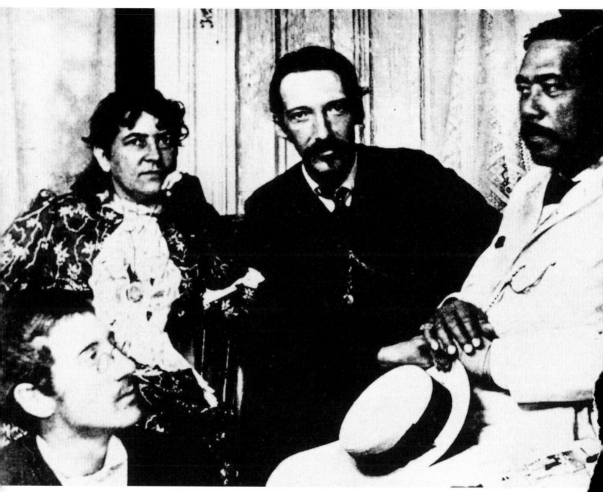

The Stevenson family entertaining a South Seas king aboard their yacht.

Louis cared about the people
on Samoa, too, and
they cared about him.

Sometimes they visited him.
Sometimes the children
danced on his lawn.

The Stevensons and their Samoan friends

Family photographs of the Stevensons and
their friends at their home in Samoa

One day in 1894, Louis was
helping Fanny with dinner.
All at once, he felt
a terrible pain in his head.
Then he passed out.

Robert Louis Stevenson
died that night.
He was only 44.

Louis had said that he
wanted to be buried
at the top of the mountain
behind his house.
So his Samoan friends
carried his body there.

Robert Louis Stevenson's grave at the top of the mountain

Later, they put a stone
on Louis' grave.
On it is carved a poem
that Louis wrote:

"This be the verse you 'grave for me:
Here he lies where he longed to be;
Home is the sailor, home from the sea,
And the hunter home from the hill."

Important Dates

1850   November 13—Born in Edinburgh, Scotland, to Margaret and Thomas Stevenson

1867   Entered Edinburgh University

1871   Declared himself a writer

1879   *Travels with a Donkey* published

1880   Married Fanny Osbourne

1883   *Treasure Island* published in book form

1885   *A Child's Garden of Verses* published

1886   *Kidnapped* and *The Strange Case of Dr. Jekyll and Mr. Hyde* published

1888   Began journey to the South Sea islands

1891   Settled in home in Samoa

1894   December 3—Died in Samoa

INDEX

Page numbers in boldface type indicate illustrations.

PHOTO CREDITS

ABOUT THE AUTHOR

Carol Greene has degrees in English literature and musicology. She has worked in international exchange programs, as an editor, and as a teacher of writing. She now lives in Webster Groves, Missouri, and writes full-time. She has published more than 100 books, including those in the Childrens Press Rookie Biographies series.